Kippen Parish Church

KIPPEN WALKS

A Pictorial Guide to Local Walks & Places of Interest

by

Steven McEwan

Contents

Introduction

Explore the breathtaking countryside of Kippen and its stunning surroundings with this informative guidebook. Immerse yourself in the rich history, natural beauty, and culture of this charming village, located just ten miles west of Stirling, Scotland. Kippen is a delightful gem nestled amidst the rolling Gargunnock and Fintry Hills, providing visitors with unparalleled views of the majestic Carse of Forth.

The first part of the book presents six walking routes that start at the Kippen Memorial Cross located in the heart of the village. Ranging in length from two to eleven miles, these routes guide readers through the picturesque woodlands, trails, hills, and quaint villages surrounding Kippen. The second part of the book highlights local points of interest, including historic buildings, pubs, and shops located within Kippen.

This guidebook is your key to unlocking the treasures that Kippen has to offer and is a must-have for any traveler who wants to experience some of the very best of Scotland's villages.

Kippen Memorial Cross on Main Street

Drawings

Part 1

Part 2

Map Key

Road

Walking route

Footpath

Buildings

Woodland

Signpost

Fields

Start and Finish

River

Part One: Walks

The Wheelbed outside The Smiddy, Rennies Loan. Used for the creation of wooden cartwheels.

1. Broich Trail – 2.4 mi

2. Redbrae Wood – 3.2 mi

3. Dasher Trail – 3.2 mi

4. Arnprior – 7.2 mi

5. Old Military Road – 7.7 mi

6. Carleatheran – 11 mi

1: Broich Trail

Distance: 2.4mi   Time: 1hr

This walk follows the old Fintry road and leads through woodland alongside the Broich burn before crossing the Arngomery field. The return route follows the back walk, which connects to Rennies Loan.

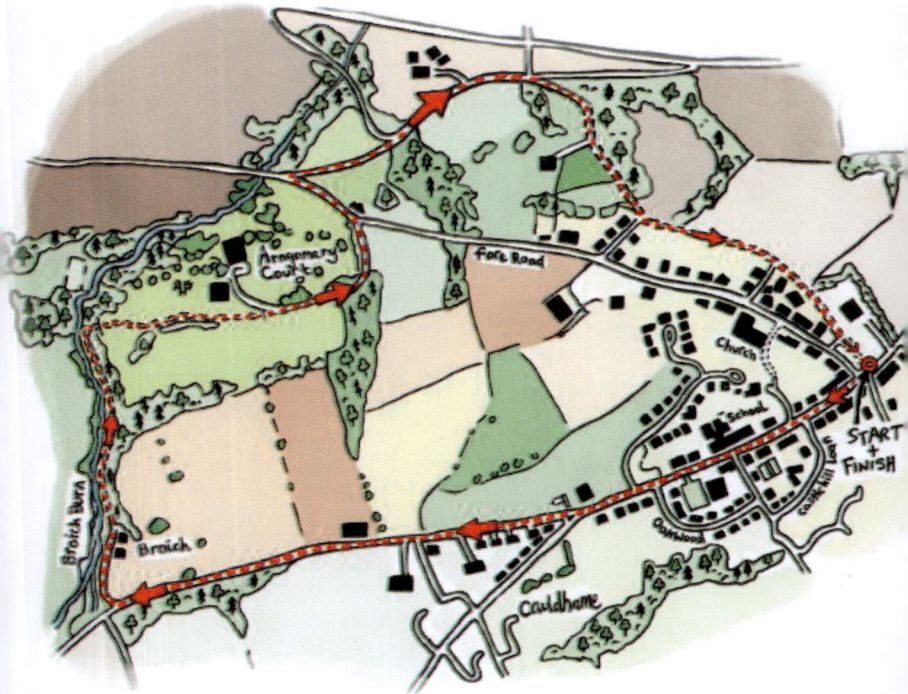

Begin your journey at Kippen cross and set off up the Main Street, taking in the charming sights and sounds of this historic village. Go past the primary school and then the car garage until you reach a breathtaking north-facing viewpoint. Take in panoramic views of the Carse of Forth, with stunning hills such as Ben Lomond, Ben Ledi, and Ben Vorlich.

Viewpoint – Trossachs (Northwest)

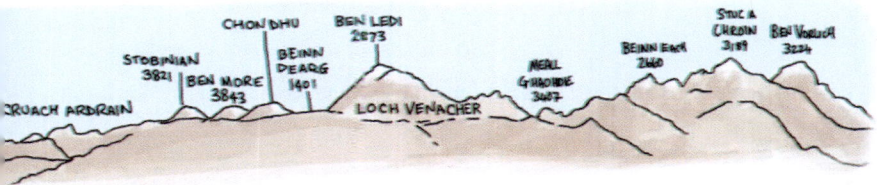

Viewpoint – Trossachs (Northeast)

Ascend the hill until you arrive at a fork in the road marked by a signpost pointing to the village of Fintry. Take the road to the right and amble along for roughly half a mile, until you reach Broich Burn crossroad. Take a sharp right turn and follow the road which runs parallel to the burn.

View from Point End, Fintry road

Proceed down this road until you reach a small row of houses. From there, continue ahead onto the woodland path and follow it downhill until it leads to an open field. Cross the field by staying on the well-trodden path and keep an eye out for a bench made from a tree on your left. To continue onward, follow the same trodden path across the field and then proceed straight down the driveway that leads to Arngomery court.

13

Tree bench near Arngomery Court

After reaching Fore Road, turn left and head downhill, then take the first right turn just before the bridge. This road will take you past a couple of farmhouses and then turn right before gradually ascending to Kippen on an old dirt track road. Follow this road for half a mile until you reach Rennie's Loan, which will lead you back to Kippen Cross.

14

2: Redbrae Woods

Distance: 3.25mi   Time: 1.5hrs

Uncover the enchantment of Redbrae Woods, then meander back to the village via Cauldhame.

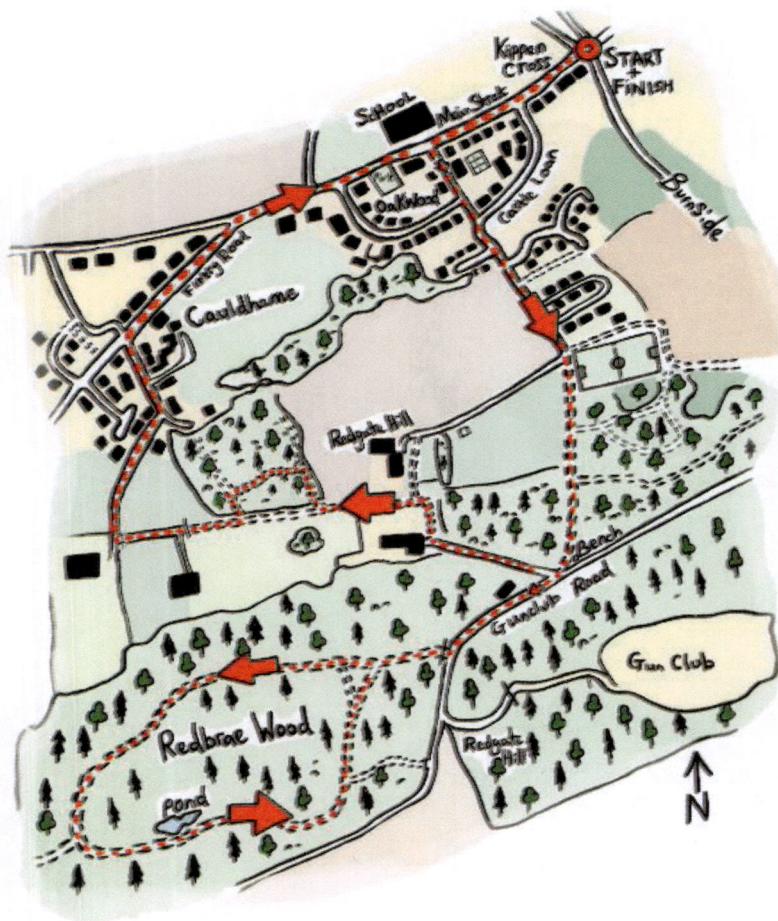

15

Starting from Kippen Cross, walk up the Main Street and when you are almost past the Primary school, take the left road signposted "Oakwood". Follow this road straight down, and it will eventually lead you to a football pitch.

Path to football pitch

After reaching the football pitch, continue straight towards the woods and join a dirt path leading up a steep hill. At the top of the hill you will find a bench and a road junction. Take the road uphill and be on the lookout for the entrance to the woodland walk, which is just after the first bend on the road. Follow the path as it loops around Redbrae woods and it will eventually bring you back to the entrance to the woods.

Redbrae Woods

After leaving Redbrae woods, return to the bench downhill and take the left road that leads to a house. Follow this road to the right onto a rough track and continue straight, joining a dirt path. Look for an entrance to Redgate woods, which will briefly take you off the path before returning you to it a little further up.

Keep following the dirt path until you reach a large gate at the end. Turn right and follow the road until you reach Fintry road. Turn right again and continue down this street until you reach Kippen Cross.

Fintry Road, Cauldhame.

18

3: Dasher Trail

Distance: 3.2mi   Time: 1.5hrs

Indulge in the spectacular views of the Trossachs as you journey to the eastern side of the village. On your return, take the scenic route through Boquhan Burn and Dasher Farm, and make your way back in style.

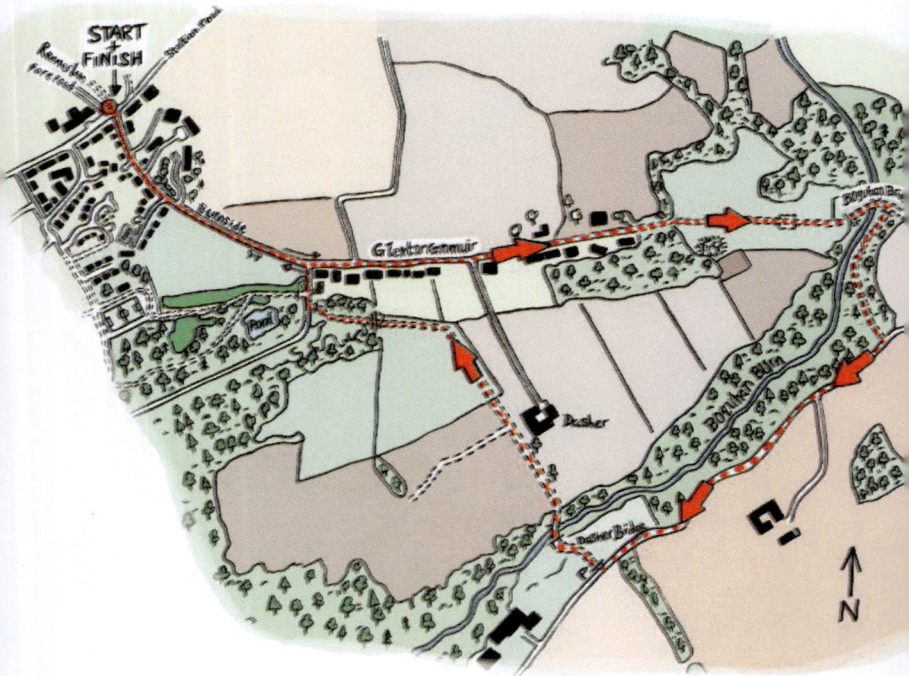

To begin, head east from Kippen Cross along Burnside Road, which is located directly across from the bus stop. Continue straight up this street, passing all the houses, until you reach a road with fields on both sides. Follow this road as it leads you to Kennel Cottage.

Kennel Cottage, Burnside Road

After Kennel Cottage, continue straight along the road through Glenterran. The road will take you down a hill and lead you to a gated field. Follow the well-trodden path across the field to reach another gate and the Boquhan bridge.

Boquhan Bridge

After crossing the Boquhan bridge, take a sharp right and climb over the gate to enter Dasher wood, which is signposted as a public path. Follow the dirt path up a steep hill through the woods until you come out on a country road. Turn right and follow the road for about half a mile until you reach a gated entrance on your right, signposted as "Public path Kippen."

View North West, towards Dasher Bridge and Farm.

21

Follow the sign towards Kippen and take the meandering farm track that leads you to Dasher bridge.

Dasher Bridge

After crossing Dasher bridge, continue straight up the red sandstone hill until you reach a gated field. Enter the field and follow the well-trodden path, which will lead you down a hill and then curves left towards the woodland. Pass through a gate and continue along the path until you reach the road. Turn right onto the road, and shortly you'll reach a T junction at Kennel Cottage. Turn left and continue straight until it brings you back to the starting point at Kippen Cross.

4: Arnprior

Distance: 7mi   Time: 2.5 hrs

Venture towards the neighboring village of Arnprior to the west of Kippen and immerse yourself in the breathtaking views of the Trossachs and its stunning countryside.

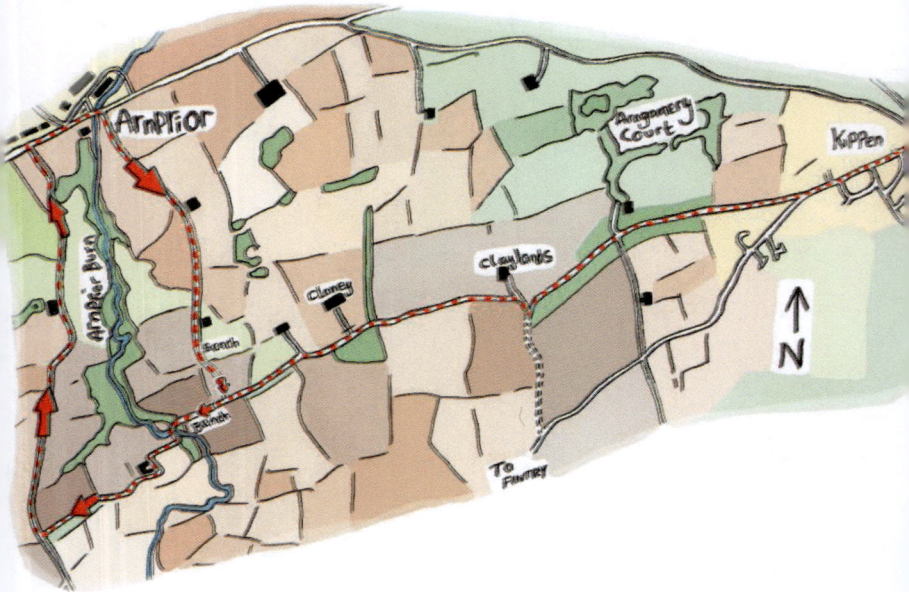

23

Begin at Kippen Cross and proceed up Main Street, passing the primary school and car garage. Keep going uphill until you come across a Y junction that has a sign indicating the direction for Fintry. Choose the right-hand path at the junction and follow it as it winds its way through the countryside for nearly three miles. Along the way, you will pass by Claylands & Clancy Farms, and then you'll come across a bench that provides a scenic view of the Trossachs.

View towards Arnprior over fields

Proceed along the same road, which descends a hill and crosses a bridge before ascending again to another farmhouse. Follow the road around the farmhouse and then directly to a T

24

junction. Turn right onto the road that goes downhill and after about a mile, it will join with the village of Arnprior.

View West near Arnprior

Cross the street to reach the pavement and turn right, walking along the main street. As you cross a bridge, you will see a road on your right. Follow this road uphill for a mile until you arrive at a T junction.

Arnprior looking East

Arnprior fields

At the T junction, take a left to join the same road you were on earlier. Continue this road all the way back to Kippen, as before, staying on the road until you reach Kippen Cross, which will take approximately three miles.

5: Old Military Road

Distance: 7.7mi   Time: 2.5hrs

This route heads East, tracing the old military road towards Gargunnock village. This journey offers a mix of country paths and roads, with just some field crossing, leading downhill towards Gargunnock Village. On the return, you will take a slightly different route, passing by the Old Leckie farm.

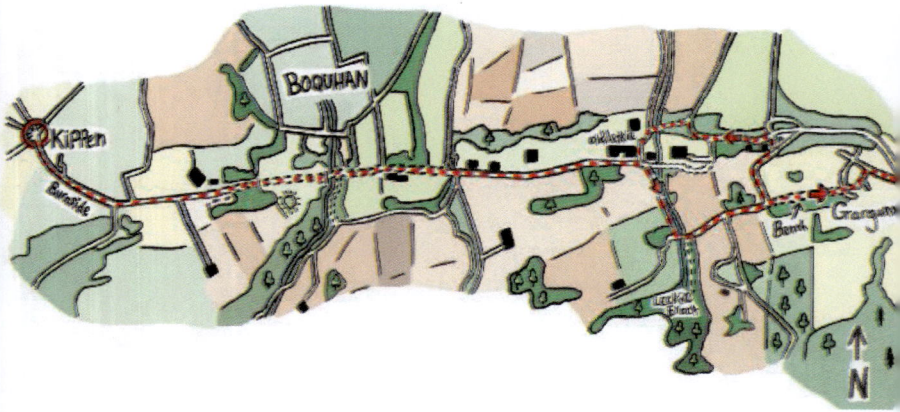

Starting at Kippen cross, proceed east along Burnside Road. On the opposite side of the bus stop, you will see a sign for Burnside on the wall. Ascend the uphill road, leading to a scenic path flanked by fields and a bench that offers views of the Trossach hills. Continue straight ahead, passing by Kennel Cottage and staying on the road that leads to Glentirranmuir. Enjoy the decent towards which will bring you to a kissing gate. Cross the field along the trodden path to reach Boquhan bridge.

Farm building near Boquham

After passing the houses, continue straight for another mile until you reach a crossroad with the stables of Old Leckie farm. Take the road on the right, which has a sign indicating Gargunnock at 1.3 miles, and follow it until you arrive at a T junction.

At the T junction, take a left turn and continue on this road until you reach a woodland path with a sign for, "The Beeches". Follow this path as it leads you into Gargunnock.

Upon reaching Gargunnock, cross the road and follow the path until you come to the first left turn, which leads you out to the main street. Turn right and head down the main street to find the Gargunnock Inn.

The Gargunnock Inn

To return to Kippen, retrace your steps to the "Beeches" sign from Gargunnock Main Street. Turn right at the sign, keep left around the farm, and continue to the Watson house. Take the downhill road to your right, then turn left and follow the dirt path to a road. Turn left and continue until you reach the crossroads at the Old Leckie Farm. Turn right and follow the signpost for Kippen for 2.6 miles to return to Kippen Cross.

6: Carleatheran

Distance: 11mi   Time: 4hrs

Enjoy a breathtaking countryside journey to the summit of Lees Hill, passing through Stronend's crags and Boquhan Burn. Admire panoramic views of Trossachs, Stirling, and the Spout of Ballochleam waterfall while driving on countryside roads.

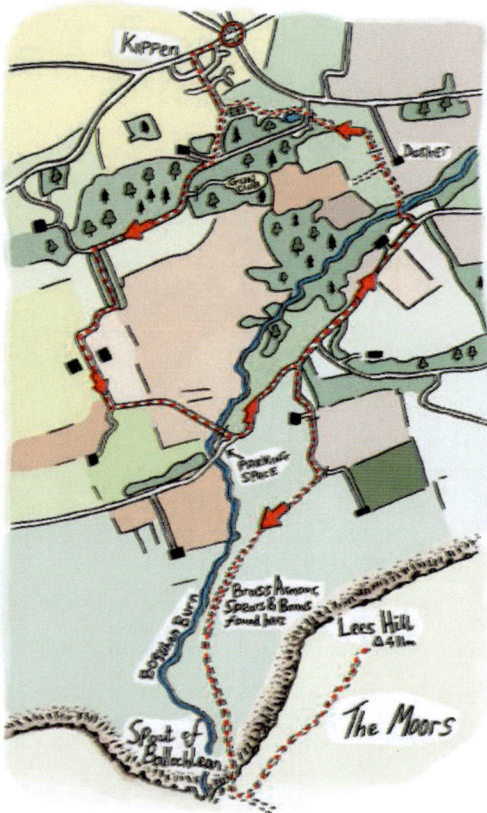

31

Starting at Kippen Cross, head up Main Street and turn left onto the road signposted "Oakwood" after passing the primary school. Follow the rough track to the football pitch and keep going straight, taking the footpath to the right of the pitch into the woods and up a steep hill. At the top of the hill, you'll find a bench and continuing along the road, you'll pass the entrance to the gun club on your left. As the road bends to the right, enjoy views of the Gargunnock hills.

View near the gun club towards Gargunnock hills

At a junction with a farm gate ahead, turn left and descend on the winding road to a farm. Pass through the farm and take the left farm road downhill, going through two gates and crossing a bridge. After the bridge, take the left road and continue for a mile until you reach a right turn sig-posted "Ballochlean".

Take the farm track, passing a farm on your right. Proceed through a series of gates. At the next split in the road, turn right through the gate. The path curves around the base of the hills and ascends steeply to the Spout of Ballochleam.

Entrance to Ballochleam

33

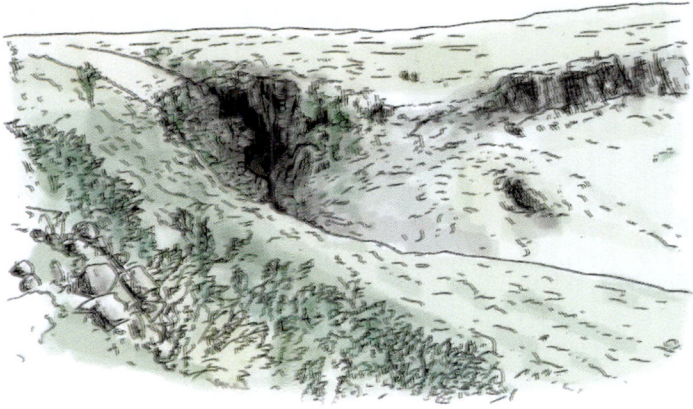

The Spout of Ballochleam

After reaching the top of the climb, you will see an information sign about the moor. Follow the path by turning left, which leads to the Lees Hill summit. Stay on the path to avoid boggy areas. At a fork, keep right, and continue until you reach a small cairn and a wooden gate. The track becomes easier to follow, leading to the trig point

Trig point lees Hill

34

surrounded by a large cairn. The rocks in the cairn are part of an ancient burial chamber.

To return to Kippen, descend the hill, pass the farm, and turn right at the Ballochlean sign. Look for the "public path" signpost by the farm on the left and follow the winding path to Dasher bridge. Ascend the red sandstone hill, go through the gated field and head straight, with the wire fence on the right. Descend the hill that curves left towards the woodland path, pass through the gate, and turn right then left to enter the woodland walk. Follow the path straight, passing the pond, until you reach the football pitch. Take the entrance on your right to return to Kippen.

The pond

Part Two: Places of Interest

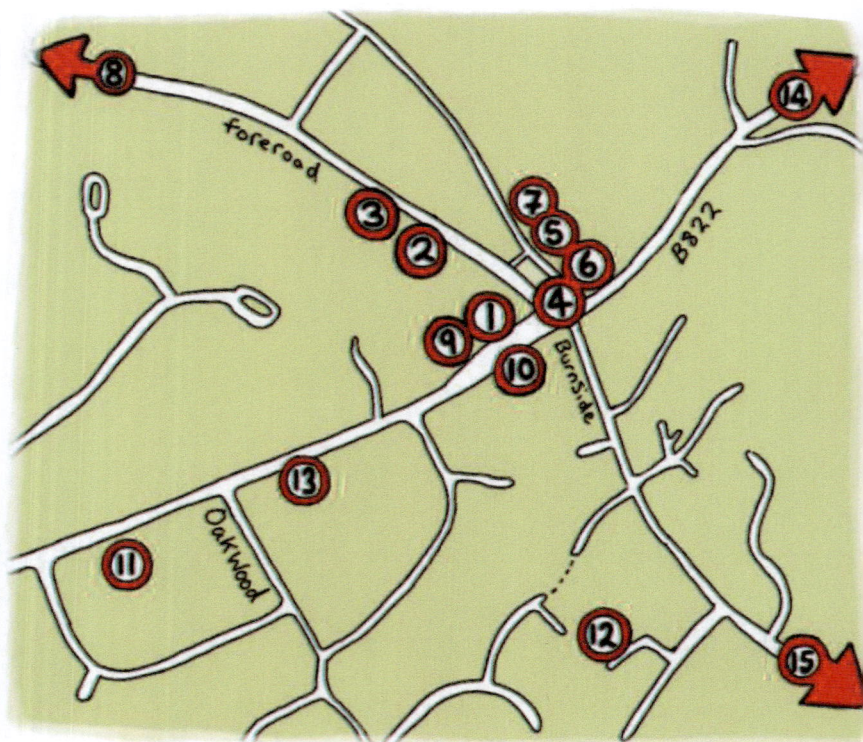

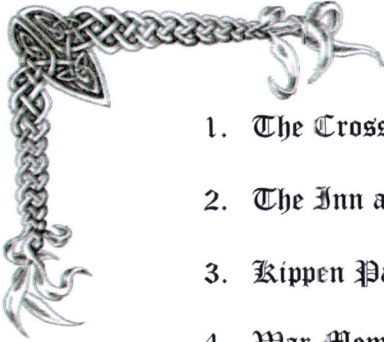

1. The Cross Keys

2. The Inn at Kippen

3. Kippen Parish Church

4. War Memorial

5. Old Smiddy

6. Ruin of The Old Kirk

7. Black Bull inn

8. Kippen Cemetery

9. Rhubarb Lime

10. McNichols Store

11. Kippen Playpark

12. The Reading Rooms

13. The Woodhouse

14. The Pond

1: 𝕿he 𝕮ross 𝕶eys -1703
Main Street

The Cross Keys is more than just an Inn - it's a destination for foodies and pub favorites alike. Whether you're in the mood for traditional fare or something more modern and experimental, the standards and specials served side by side until 9 pm are sure to delight your taste buds. And with its open-plan design and lively atmosphere, the bar, lounge, and restaurant seamlessly merge into a spirited hub of village life, where locals, families, and food enthusiasts gather to revel in the unique ambiance and conviviality that The Cross Keys has to offer.

41

2: The Inn at Kippen

Foreroad

The Inn at Kippen offers a restaurant serving fresh seafood and locally sourced meats, as well as a selection of Scottish ales and whiskies. It's a great place to stay for a romantic getaway or family vacation. The function room has beautiful views and is perfect for weddings, business meetings, or parties. The inn has all the amenities you need to make your event memorable.

3: Kippen Parish Church

Foreroad

Nestled in the heart of Kippen village, the Kippen Parish Church was erected in 1827, serving as a beacon of faith and community to locals and visitors alike. Its striking stone exterior and elegant yet simple interior showcases the traditional Scottish architecture that has enraptured many. While the church has been updated with modern amenities, it still holds onto its historic charm.

With regular Sunday services and special holiday events, the church continues to offer spiritual nourishment and welcomes visitors to explore its rich history.

43

4: War Memorial
Main Street

The War Memorial was erected 1920, and is a poignant
tribute to the local residents who made the ultimate sacrifice during
World War I and World War II. Serving as a beacon of hope,
healing, and unity for the community, the War Memorial holds a
special place in the hearts of locals and visitors alike, especially on
Remembrance Day, as it stands as a solemn symbol of remembrance,
respect, and gratitude for those who gave their lives in service to
their country.

5: Old Smiddy
Rennies Loan

The Old Smiddy is a historic building dating back to the 18th century and was originally used as a blacksmith's workshop. It now serves as a museum that showcases the village's rural heritage and the skills of its craftsmen. Owned by the National Trust, it is open to the public on select days, allowing visitors to see the interior of a traditional blacksmiths, as well as learn more about the village's farming and agricultural history.

6: Ruin of the Old Kirk
Main Street

The Ruin of Old Kirk is a hauntingly beautiful site that tells a tale of the village's spiritual past. Despite its rich history, the Old Kirk fell into disrepair over the years and now stands as a picturesque ruin, with the chancel, nave, and part of the tower still visible. The church bell is dated 1618. The surrounding churchyard is equally fascinating, with numerous historic graves and monuments, providing a glimpse into the village's past. The site is currently closed, access to be requested via Stirling Council Cemetery Office.

7: Black Bull Inn
Rennies Loan

The Black Bull Inn, a 17th-century building, was a thriving inn and public house in its early days. After undergoing extensive restoration and refurbishment by the National Trust for Scotland, it has been transformed into a beautiful private residence. Although The Black Bull Inn is not open to the public, its impressive presence in the heart of Kippen stands as a reminder of the village's storied past and cultural heritage.

8: Kippen Cemetery
Fintry Road

Kippen Cemetery is a historic burial ground situated on a hillside overlooking the village, and it has been a place of burial for the local community for over 50 years.

The cemetery is a peaceful and reflective space, with many well-maintained graves and monuments dating back to the 19th century. It is also surrounded by beautiful Scottish countryside, providing a serene and tranquil atmosphere.

9: 𝕽𝖍𝖚𝖇𝖆𝖗𝖇 𝕷𝖎𝖒𝖊
Main Street

Rhubarb Lime is a charming shop that offers an array of artisanal food and drink products, including delicious cheeses, delectable chocolates, and delightful preserves. The store prides itself on its carefully curated selection of distinctive, top-quality products that are sourced from local artisans and independent producers. In addition to the outstanding products, Rhubarb Lime is also known for its welcoming and friendly environment.

10: McNichols Store
Main Street

A convenience store that offers a wide range of everyday essentials such as groceries, snacks, toiletries, household items, and postal services. Centrally located in the heart of the village, it serves as a convenient and reliable stop for both locals and visitors.

50

11: Kippen Playpark
Fintry Road

Kippen Playpark is a well-maintained and spacious park that offers play opportunities for children of all ages. The park features various equipment, such as swings, slides, climbing frames, and a roundabout, among others. Children can also play ball games on the large grassy area, while families can relax and have a picnic on the benches and picnic table provided.

13: The Reading Rooms
Fintry Road

The Reading Rooms is a historic building that has been lovingly restored and transformed into a modern space for local events, workshops, and exhibitions. It is also used for community meetings and educational events. The building still retains many of its historic features, including the original stone facade and large windows, giving it a unique and charming character.

14: The Woodhouse
Kippen Station Roundabout

The Woodhouse is a popular destination for locals and travelers alike, and is a must-visit for anyone looking for a taste of Scotland's rich culinary heritage. The restaurant features a menu that showcases the best of local, seasonal produce, including meat from Skinner of Kippen, a renowned local butcher. In addition to its delicious food, The Woodhouse has an outdoor seating area with a garden and patio that are perfect for al fresco dining during the warmer months.

15: Pond

Burnside

The pond, located near the football pitch in Kippen, is a charming and serene body of water that is a favorite spot for both locals and visitors. It is surrounded by verdant greenery and is a haven for various species of wildlife, including ducks, swans, and other waterfowl, that can be observed swimming and nesting in the area.

kippenwalks@gmail.com

facebook/Kippenwalks.co.uk

Notes

Printed in Great Britain
by Amazon